The Legend of

TE TUNA

The Legend of

TE TUNA

RICHARD ADAMS

Illustrated by **Ul de Rico**

Sidgwick & Jackson
LONDON

This edition first published in Great Britain in 1986
by Sidgwick and Jackson Limited

Originally published in a limited edition in 1982
by Sylvester and Orphanos, Los Angeles, California, USA

ISBN 0-283-99393-6

Printed in Italy by
Amilcare Pizzi, s.p.a., Milan
for Sidgwick and Jackson Limited
1 Tavistock Chambers, Bloomsbury Way
London WC1A 2SG

To
VERA VON DER HEYDT,
with love and gratitude

Note on Pronunciation

Before the coming of the Europeans during the latter half of the eighteenth century, the Polynesian Islands were a civilization without metal and without a written language. Today, a great many Polynesians still get by very well without reading or writing. Written Polynesian was 'constructed' by Europeans, and consists simply of phonetic approximation to the spoken words. Spoken Polynesian has five vowels and eight consonants. Naturally, the vowels get plenty of use. For example, 'Fa' means soap; 'Faa' means a ham sandwich; and 'Faaa' is the name of Tahiti's airport.

The Legend of Te Tuna uses the spelling of proper names commonly accepted throughout the Polynesian Triangle. There are a few diphthongs (for example, 'Maui' is *'Mow-ee')* but, for the most part, all vowels are pronounced as single syllables; 'Huahine', for instance, is *'Hoo-ahhee-nee',* 'Tuamotu' is *'Tew-a-mo-tew',* and 'Kamake' is *'Kam-ah-kee';* while (perhaps best of all), 'Fariua-a-Makitua' is *'Far-ee-oo-ah ah Mau-kit-oo-ah'.*

I have thought it best to include this brief note, since in several instances correct pronunciation is necessary to the scansion of the lines.

R. G. A.

I

Deep in the seas, deep in the southern seas
The coral palace of Te Tuna lies
Beneath the ocean. Far above, the breeze
Whitens the crests, the fulmar petrel flies
On its great journeys and the gulls' sharp cries
Quicken the isles. Below, the poison-spined,
Bloat stonefish waits, the squid's enormous eyes
Pierce the cold gloom and nameless fishes, blind
With ancient darkness shun their own devouring kind.

Deep in the seas, deep in the southern seas
The coral palace of Te Tuna lies
Beneath the ocean . . . .

II

This is his realm, the lord of Ocean, he,
The terrible Te Tuna, giant eel,
Fanged as with spears. Around him, silently,
His supple, luminous attendants steal
Upon their errands. Dark weeds half-conceal
Him, coiled about the amber that enthrones
His mottled bulk. Drowsy, he turns to feel
The icy currents gliding on the stones
Or scratch his flanks upon a rack of human bones.

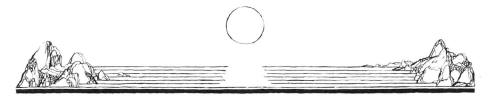

III

But who is this that sits upon his right,
More beautiful than darkness and the stars
Reflected from a clear lagoon at night?
Look how the dim, sea-filtered sunbeam bars
Her belly with fine ripples white as scars
Long-healed! This is warm Hina of the Sky,
His consort; but a sidelong frowning mars
Her beauty. Discontent has made her sly.
She frets, her passion for Te Tuna all gone by.

IV

She kneels and speaks. "I will go now, my lord,
"To seek your food." Swiftly his white eyes burn
  Upon her, penetrating like a sword,
In cold desire. "And when shall you return?"
  She answers, with a look of unconcern,
"I needs must be some time. Far out to sea
  "I'll go; enquire about the isles to learn
"Where the food's best, then cook it skilfully."
"Go, then, my heart, that sooner you'll return to me."

But who is this that sits upon his right,
More beautiful than darkness and the stars
Reflected from a clear lagoon at night?

V

Quickly she's gone. Up through the tumbling seas
　　Her brown limbs waver, up into the spume
　　Along the reefs, where mermaid-manatees
Suckle their young. Wind-wafted, the perfume
　　Of frangipani carries, from the gloom
Of humid woods where, pendent in the shade
　　The red hibiscus thrusts from out the bloom
Its long, erectile stamen. Half-dismayed,
She trembles, of her own voluptuous thoughts afraid.

VI

Then, taking heart, boldly she makes her way,
Hot for a lover, to the jagged peaks
Of northern Hatutu; thence to the bay
Of Mangareva, and the peopled creeks
Along Tahiti's coast. Yearning, she seeks
A mate among the green glades of Morea,
And lifting up her clear young voice, she speaks
Of joyous, shameless love to whom may hear
From Huahine's top to sacred Raiatea.

VII

Bronze-gold she was as cassia on the tree.
Of all who saw or heard her, not a man
But kindled, burning with cupidity:
Ay, and with fear of that leviathan
The fanged Te Tuna, he, more dreaded than
Lightning and wave, typhoon or hurricane.
They fled from her, till, weary, she began
To weep with unassuaged desire, and pain
Of her broad loins that longed for lover's ease in vain.

Bronze-gold she was as cassia on the tree.
Of all who saw or heard her, not a man
But kindled, burning with cupidity . . . .

VIII

Maui it was–that fisher-up of lands,
Stealer of fire and raiser of the sky–
Maui–he heard her, where the grainy sands
Of occidental Bora-Bora lie
Below green hills. Stealing, and peeping sly
Between the leaves, he watched her drawing near.
His mother, Hua-Hega, stood near by:
She came to him and whispered in his ear,
"Go, take that woman for thyself and have no fear."

"His mother, Hua-Hega, stood near by:
"She came to him and whispered in his ear,
"Go, take that woman for thyself and have no fear."

IX

Lazy and warm the calm of the lagoon;
Lazy and warm the huge stars of the night;
The limbs entwined in sleep before the moon
Has crossed the zenith. Swift the morning, bright
With candle-bush and jasmine, and delight
Of green, cascading streams among the ferns.
Crowned with tiare-blossom, fragant-white,
Warm Hina laughs as Maui's passion burns
Her glowing limbs, consumes itself and yet returns.

Lazy and warm the calm of the lagoon;
Lazy and warm the huge stars of the night . . . .

X

And she forgets that dimness where the giant,
Unsleeping lord Te Tuna, he, waits still;
Nor sees in memory those grim, compliant
Sea-warriors moving darkly through the chill
And sluggish depths to carry out his will.
Lovers believe they have no enemies
While all the forests whisper, each green hill
Cries out with jealousy and every breeze
Betrays their secret through and under all the seas.

XI

Te Tuna learned that news. In bitter anger
He cursed—as even gods had cursed—the name
Of Maui-Tikitiki-Ataranga,
Hero of cunning stratagems, that same
Who fished the islands up and first stole flame
Out of the sky. With barbed fangs gaping wide
For vengeance, up between the seas he came,
His four chief warriors swimming at his side.
Westward they swam and stopped for neither night nor tide.

XII

They came to Bora's reef at dawn. The ocean
Boiled into turbulence. The sky grew red
As new-spilled blood. The treetops, in commotion,
Bent, cracked and toppled in the wind that sped
Across the island. All but Maui fled
In terror as Te Tuna rose to view
Beyond the coral, his gigantic head
Snarling, white-eyed, above his retinue.
The wave they rode on struck the reef and broke it through.

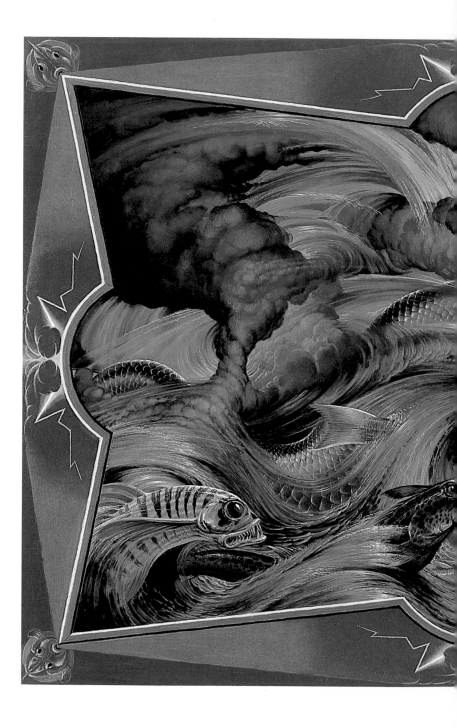

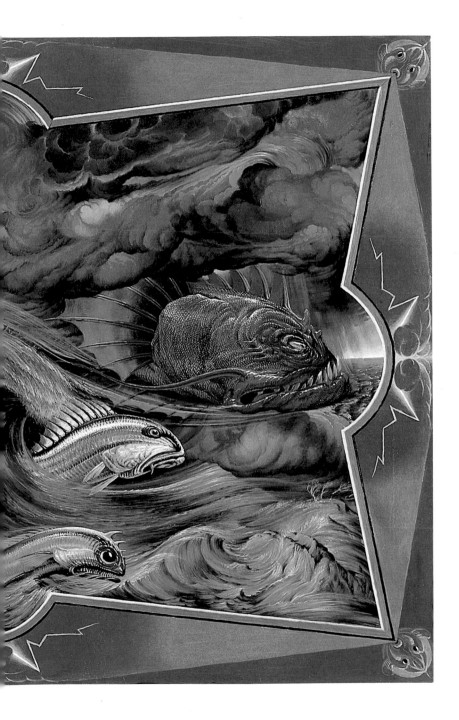

*. . . With barbed fangs gaping wide
For vengeance, up between the seas he came,
His four chief warriors swimming at his side . . . .*

XIII

Already that great billow had begun
Its surging course to overthrow the land,
When the first rays of the new-risen sun
Showed Maui standing naked on the sand,
Alone and waiting. As he raised his hand
The wave receded till the ocean floor
Lay bare, and not a warrior could withstand
Its swift recoil. Te Tuna and his four
Fierce henchmen lay thrown down and vanquished on the shore.

XIV

Strong Pupu-vai-e-noa, he fell dead.
Porporo-tu-huaga lay pierced through.
Maga-vai-i-e-rire's entrails bled
Upon the coral, mingling with the blue
And crimson weeds. These three the hero slew:
But one—Toke-a-Kura he was called—
Turned tail too fast for Maui to pursue
Or capture. Through the broken reef he crawled,
Then plunged and disappeared through depths of emerald.

XV

Te Tuna Maui spared. They went together
To Maui's home; and there, the tales relate,
Te Tuna dwelt; but not a tale tells whether
He wept to see warm Hina, once his mate,
Reject him, whether he sustained his hate
    Or if by sudden impulse he was led
    To challenge Maui. Only, soon or late,
They tell, there came an evening when he said
Maui and he must fight again till one was dead.

. . . As he raised his hand
The wave receded . . . .

XVI

Who shall withstand the great Orea eel?
Mounting in sinuous coils, he swings and sways
About his enemy from head to heel,
Chanting an ocean-woven spell, to daze
And fascinate him. Maui meets his gaze
Impassively. "See, I contract, grow small.
"I enter you and thread the close-coiled maze
"Of your intestines, Maui. You were tall
"And strong, Maui, but you shall wither, droop and fall."

XVII

And he has vanished into Maui's loins.
The seas hush, the breeze drops and all around
Is silence. Maui stands where the beach joins
The water. All night long he made no sound
And gave no tremor as Te Tuna wound
His course within. The eastern sky grew pale,
The new sun rose, and still he stood his ground,
Until at fainting noon–so runs the tale–
Te Tuna reappeared, for he could not prevail.

XVIII

And now he faces Maui on the sand,
Forsaken of his love, and of his art,
And of his ocean warriors. He must stand
Alone, for Maui to contract and dart
Into his body, even to the heart.
He felt an agony along his side
And all his sinewy coils were rent apart.
The white eyes stared, the great fangs shivered wide
And clenched, and on the beach Te Tuna fell and died.

. . . and his gift shall be
The staple of the isles for evermore,
"Husk of sea-green, arisen from the sea."

XIX

Maui steps forth. Your enemy lies dead
Before you, trickster, nooser of the sun,
Fisher of isles! Go, take her to your bed
Again, warm Hina of the Sky. There's none
To stay you now. No, he is carrion
For crabs and gulls. Not even his cold ghost
Shall vex your dreams. Cut off his head, and run
Quick home and show it. Caper there, and boast,
And bury it beside your dwelling's corner-post.

XX

Two months are passed. The Southern Cross hangs bright
In the spring sky and the terns make their way
Southward once more. One jasmine-scented night
Maui lies idly gazing at a ray
Of moonlight on the floor, and his eyes stray
With it towards the corner-post; and there
A shoot has sprung out of the sand, a spray
Of leaves. His mother, watching, sees him stare
And tremble and fall down upon his face in prayer.

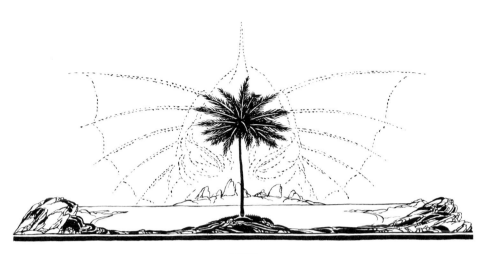

XXI

"Have no dismay, my son. It is a blessing
"Bestowed by him who was thine enemy.
"He whom thou slew is now at peace, possessing
"The sky and ocean, and a heart set free
"From lovers' sorrow; and his gift shall be
"The staple of the isles for evermore,
"Husk of sea-green, arisen from the sea."
Then, at his mother's bidding, Maui swore
To tend that plant and nurture it beside their door.

This is that tree by which the islands live . . . .

XXII

This is that tree by which the islands live:
That bounteous tree whose sea-green husks provide
Both food and drink: whose fibrous wrappings give
Stout cloth for cleaning-rags, whose leaves are dried
For thatch, whose scooped-out shells are set aside
For cups and eating-vessels. Every child
Knows of the lord Te Tuna, him who died
At Maui's hands on Bora-Bora's wild,
Green shore and by his gift to men was reconciled.

XXIII

My guest, if they should ask thee, in thy far,
North-lying land, who told this tale to thee,
    'Twas Fariua-a-Makitua,
    The Tuamotu chief, whom Kamake,
Most learned of the sages, taught. And see!
The words are true, for since they were begun
    Three coconuts have fallen—one for me
    And one for him who listened; ay, and one
For him who told the tale—and now the tale is done.

.